A GUIDE TO THE INTERNET

FOR HUMAN RIGHTS DEFENDERS

by Becky Hogge

First published in 2014
by Barefoot Publishing Limited
72 Edburton Avenue
Brighton BN1 6EL

Edited by: Dixie Hawtin
Typeset by: Becky Hogge

© Becky Hogge, 2014

All illustrations © Tactical Studios

The moral right of the author has been asserted

ISBN: 978-0-9930999-0-8

"The same rights that people have offline
must also be protected online."

United Nations Human Rights Council, 2012

The internet is the defining technology of our age. Sometimes gradually, sometimes dramatically, it is shifting power relationships in every aspect of our lives, from commerce to politics, from education to art. With these shifts come new opportunities in the field of human rights, but also new threats.

The internet empowers people by placing the means to access and disseminate information directly in their hands. It grants even those with only a modest level of technical skill the ability to bypass state censorship. Where once the power to communicate with a wide audience was monopolised by elites, the internet allows ordinary people to raise their voices against injustice, incompetence and ignorance. It presents all of us with new ways to organise ourselves, to make a difference in our communities and in our societies. It paves the way for new digital services with the potential to put prosperity in the hands of the world's poorest. And it has the capacity to offer the socially marginalised, the physically disabled, the visually impaired and many other disadvantaged groups new channels of communication and expression, free from intolerance or impediment. The internet provides opportunities for advancing human development and human rights. Already, we can see the possibilities.

In Kenya, citizens used email and their mobile phones to send messages about political violence they had witnessed.

These messages were gathered together on a website – Ushahidi – that was able to present a picture of levels of violence during the 2007-2008 post-election crisis.

In Tunisia, as thousands of people took to the streets to protest against the economic and human rights hardships suffered under a decades-old regime, activists shared details of police movements and of demonstrations on Facebook and Twitter, and posted videos live from the streets to YouTube and DailyMotion – videos that Al Jazeera beamed back onto Tunisia's television sets, stoking the revolution and spreading the news around the world.

"The internet empowers people by placing the means to access and disseminate information directly in their hands"

In Saudi Arabia, thousands of people signed an online petition calling for an end to the kingdom's ban on women driving, with dozens of women using YouTube to post videos of themselves violating the ban on a designated "Day of Women Driving", intended to put pressure on the authorities to address the issue.

Although the internet provides opportunities for human development and the advancement of human rights, it brings threats with it, too. With new forms of expression come new forms of censorship and surveillance. What's more, as communications technology spreads, uneven patterns of adoption amplify already-existing inequalities. The same features that make the internet a great way to disseminate information and rally individuals around a collective cause can also make it a great way to spread disinformation and polarise people. The fact that the computers that power the internet are able, by their very nature, to retain near-perfect records of all the online activity of all of their users means that personal privacy is fundamentally at risk as we move into the digital age.

It has never been easier for the state to locate and identify an activist who uses digital communications technology to organise and, once they are so located, to spy on, record and supress their activities. Dissidents in Egypt have given accounts of being confronted with their own private text messages during interrogation sessions under the Mubarak regime. State-sponsored hacking attacks against independent news media and human rights groups have been reported in Tunisia, Russia, China, Vietnam, Burma, Mexico, Israel, Egypt and Iran.

In 2012, the United Nations recognised the huge impact of digital technology on human rights and resolved that "The same rights that people have offline must also be protected online". This resolution reflects a hope for the future, not the present state of affairs, and this hope cannot be realised without action on the part of human rights defenders who understand the internet and the opportunities and threats it presents.

Understanding and addressing how the underlying structure of the internet, and the way it is operated and governed, affect the rights of its users is a new field – a field from which human rights expertise is currently lacking. Instead, powerful interests – mainly governments and big businesses – are being permitted to shape our digital future in key debates, treaties and deals that are happening now. Those civil society groups that are involved in these debates are fighting an unequal fight, and desperately need the diversity and depth that the human rights community brings with it.

The digital rights they are defending will be rights on which we all come to rely, even those of us who think the internet has little to do with our day-to-day work now. It is time for human rights defenders from the offline world to familiarise themselves with the internet, and prepare to defend human rights online.

AN OVERVIEW OF THIS GUIDE

To people who are used to defending human rights in the "real" world – a place geeks often refer to as IRL (In Real Life) or AFK (Away From Keyboard) – the internet can seem like a foreign language.

The aim of this guide, then, resembles that of any good travel guide: to introduce newcomers to the history, workings and culture of the virtual world and help them find the features most relevant to their concerns. It is much easier to enjoy a trip abroad when you understand a bit about your destination and speak some of the local language, and it is impossible to defend human rights online successfully without a basic understanding of the history of the internet and how it works.

The next chapter is a short introduction to what the internet is (and what it is not). Chapter Two contains a brief history of the internet, its technical development, use and governance. Chapter Three explains the different technologies that power the internet, and the actors behind them. Chapter Four introduces the various groups and institutions that either have or want a stake in internet governance, and are therefore poised to influence the future of human rights online. Chapter Five outlines the major human rights issues to look out for in the new digital world, and Chapter Six examines possible futures for networked digital communications, and their human rights implications.

You will find many technical terms as you read, but do not be put off by them. This guide is aimed at a non-technical audience, so where technical terms are included, these are in *italic* print and are explained in the extensive glossary at the end of the guide. By the time you have finished reading this guide, although you may not yet be referring to the non-virtual world using three-letter acronyms, you will be able to speak a little bit of geek yourself.

CONTENTS

WAIT, WHERE AM I?   13

HOW DID WE GET HERE?   17
Development   19
Adoption   20
Uses   20
Governance   21

ARE YOU SURE THIS THING'S WORKING?   23
The layer model   25
The physical layer   26
The code layer   30
The application layer   32
The content layer   35

CAN I SPEAK TO THE MANAGER?   39
State-level governance   45
Corporations   45
Users and digital civil society   46
Technical governance   47
The United Nations   49
Country groupings   52

WHAT A HUMAN RIGHTS ISSUE LOOKS LIKE NOW   55
Censorship   57
Surveillance   62
The global digital divide   64
Harmful content   67

STOP THIS THING, I WANT TO GET OFF! 69

Weaponisation of cyberspace 71
Internet balkanisation 72
The internet of things 73
Big data 74

GLOSSARY 77

ABOUT THE AUTHOR 93

chapter 1

WAIT, WHERE AM I?

What the internet is and is not

The internet is made up of millions of computers across the world, all connected to one another and sharing information. People talk about downloading things "from the internet" or going "onto the internet" or "online" to check facts or fetch emails. What they're really doing is using the internet to download information onto their computer from some other computer somewhere on the internet.

The internet has been called a "world of ends" and an "end-to-end network", because on the internet the stuff that matters, the smart stuff, happens at the end points, at the computers that connect to it. The computers that connect to the internet are constantly generating, storing and sharing information.

"Computers" here doesn't just mean the laptop in your bag right now. It could mean the 180,000 computer *servers*, currently running in Pineville, Oregon, that make up Facebook; it could mean the *smartphones* in the pockets of 41% of Nigerians. One day soon, it might mean your refrigerator, your car or even your bath (see Chapter Six for more on the *internet of things*).

And "information" here doesn't just mean bus timetables or research reports. Information means absolutely anything that can be translated into the computer's language of ones and zeros. That could be videos shot and uploaded live from a protest in Istanbul, or pictures of cats, or the voices of people who live halfway across the world from their families, using Skype to

15

catch up. It could be *software* updates, or malicious computer viruses. Or it could be a shaky camera recording of the latest Bollywood movie, being shared illicitly using *peer-to-peer file-sharing*.

"The internet is made up of millions of computers across the world, all connected to one another and sharing information"

The internet's end-to-end structure arises from the fact that, unlike the communications networks that came before it, the internet was not designed with one particular type of communication in mind. The *communications protocols* that allow the computers that make up the internet to connect to one another are designed to run on almost any type of physical infrastructure and to carry any type of digital information. It is this design that has made the internet so scalable and flexible, and allowed innovation online to flourish.

chapter 2

HOW DID WE GET HERE?

A short history of the internet

Many of the internet's peculiarities today are traceable to its history.

DEVELOPMENT

The origins of the internet lie in research carried out during the 1960s, much of it funded by the United States' Department of Defense, which sought to build resilient communications infrastructure using computer networks. This research led to the development of many different *packet-switching* computer networks across the United States and Europe. As these different networks flourished, ideas about joining them together were put forward. The *TCP/IP* protocol (see Chapter Three), which allows this "inter-networking", was gradually adopted and an elementary,

TIMELINE

1969: Computers in Stanford and Los Angeles connect across the ARPANET *packet-switching* network for the first time

1971: First email sent

1973: Email accounts for 75% of the traffic on ARPANET

1974: First recorded use of the word "internet"

1977: *Modem* invented, Apple II computer launched

1980: Usenet computer network communications system established

1984: *Domain Name System* created

1986: *IETF* holds its first meeting

1988: US National Science Foundation invests heavily in internet infrastructure

1990: Tim Berners-Lee proposes the *worldwide web*.

1993: John Gilmore tells Time magazine, "The internet interprets censorship as damage and routes around it"; Mosaic web *browser* launched

1995: eBay and Amazon launched

1996: John Perry Barlow writes the "Declaration of the Independence of Cyberspace"; WIPO members adopt Internet Treaties

1998: Google *search engine* launched; US enacts *DMCA*, including provisions for *intermediary liability*; China begins its "Golden Shield Project", pop-

global *"network of networks"* – the internet – was born.

ADOPTION

At first, the internet was used mainly by academic institutions, although hobbyists could use early *modems* and personal computers to log on via the telephone network. During the 1990s people started adopting the internet at a rapid pace that has not slowed since: at the beginning of the decade, about 313,000 computers were connected to the internet; by 2000 that figure was over 93 million. Today, 2.5 billion people – more than one third of the world's population – have access to the internet.

USES

Email dominated the internet for a long time after the first email was sent in 1971. During the 1980s, online forums, such as Usenet, and bulletin board systems (BBS) became widely used. During the 1990s, the *worldwide web* led to a huge increase in the amount of information available to non-technical people via the internet; this decade also saw the rise of e-commerce. Peer-to-peer filesharing, *social media*, video and *voice-over-IP* all blossomed online during the 2000s, despite the dotcom bust early in the decade. 2010 saw the first of many mass online disclosures of state secrets; these may ultimately contribute to defining the 2010s as the decade during which the internet became a major political force.

GOVERNANCE

Early internet pioneers defended the internet as a place that defied state-level regulation because of its global nature, but since the early 1990s, states and their legal systems have enacted new laws and adapted old ones to attempt to regulate internet activity. At an international level, states and civil society have looked to the United Nations (UN) to address internet governance issues and to influence the development of the globally networked world, through the UN-sponsored World Summits on the Infor-

ularly known as "The Great Firewall of China"; *ICANN* takes over core internet oversight from the US Department of Defense

2000: Dotcom bubble bursts; Europe adopts *E-Commerce Directive,* including provisions for *intermediary liability*

2001: Wikipedia launched

2003: Google buys Blogger; Skype launched; first *WSIS* summit held

2004: Facebook launched

2005: YouTube launched; second *WSIS* summit held

2006: Google buys YouTube; Twitter launched; first meeting of the *IGF*

2008: The Open Net Initiative calls internet censorship "limited"

2009: France adopts HADOPI law, including

notice and disconnection provisions

2010: *IGF* mandate is renewed until 2015; ONI says internet censorship "becoming a global norm"; WikiLeaks begins disclosure of classified US documents

2011: Freedom Online Coalition launched; IBSA calls for greater UN involvement in internet governance

2012: Mass protests prevent passing of SOPA in the US; attempt by some *ITU* members to bring aspects of internet governance under its control fails

2013: Edward Snowden leaks classified documents detailing the internet surveillance activities of the US and allied governments

mation Society (*WSIS*) in 2003 and 2005, which in turn gave rise to the Internet Governance Forum (*IGF*). Away from the scrutiny of civil society, multilateral trade negotiations and meetings of the International Telecommunications Union (*ITU*) also provide settings in which corporations and governments attempt to form internet policy.

chapter three

ARE YOU SURE THIS THING'S WORKING?

Understanding the internet

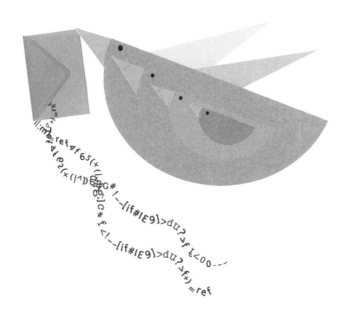

The internet is designed to run on almost any type of physical infrastructure and carry any type of information. This design has made the internet scalable and flexible, and allowed innovation online to flourish.

Having a basic grasp of how the internet works will help anyone new to defending human rights online understand more clearly the different actors and threats they encounter.

THE LAYER MODEL

One way to understand how the internet works is to think of it as a series of layers. The *physical layer*, at the bottom of the stack, contains the hardware components – computers, *routers*, *switches*, etc. – that underpin the internet. On top of this is the *code layer* (a series of *software* layers, often called the *protocol stack*, or *TCP/IP*), which defines the way applications (the third layer up) and their content (the top layer) are transported around the network.

Each of these layers works independently of the others: for example, what the *physical layer* is made up of – be it *copper wire*, *optical fibre* or radio signals – has no bearing on what type of content – voice, music, text, code –it can carry. It is this independence, together with the rigorous standardisation of the various *protocols* in the *TCP/IP protocol stack* (see The code layer section, below), that characterises the internet and makes it so

25

successful as a scalable network. For example, when you write an email (*content layer*) using Microsoft Outlook (*application layer*), and hit send, the information is encoded with a series of protocols (*code layer*) that will shape how and where it is transported. Much as the postman does not need to look inside an envelope to ascertain where a letter needs to go, so the *routers* and *switches* (*physical layer*) that make up the local and global networks across which your email travels need only look at the information encoded in the protocols specific to them. The same is true of a conversation (*content layer*) taking place over Skype (*application layer*), that is encoded and divided into *packets* (*code layer*) and routed around a global network (*physical layer*) of, among other things, the computers of other Skype users.

Although the way the internet works may be hard to grasp at first, it is important for human rights activists to have a basic understanding of it. Threats to human rights may occur in any one of these layers. Each layer is shaped by a different set of actors.

THE PHYSICAL LAYER
What is it?

The word "internet" derives from "inter-networking"(see Chapter Two): joining several different *packet-switching* communications networks together. The internet can therefore be understood as a *network of networks*. At its *physical layer*, this means the internet is made of the same stuff that communications networks are made of: *network nodes*, connected to each other by various *network connections*.

A *network node* could be a computer or computer *server*, but it could also be a piece of networking hardware, such as a *switch* (which links and routes network traffic between hosts on

REGULATION AND NETWORK OPERATORS

Network operators and *website hosts* are generally granted immunity from prosecution for the content that travels across their wires, provided they make efforts, when requested, to *block*, or remove from their *servers*, content found or alleged to be illegal or infringing. In several regions, including the US and Europe, this arrangement is codified in law and referred to as *intermediary liability*.

Market regulation mechanisms – and increasingly statutes (in Chile, Brazil and the Netherlands) – also control how much network operators are permitted to interfere with the internet traffic they carry for their own business purposes, in order to preserve the principle of *net neutrality*, the fundamental design principle of the internet as an end-to-end network (see Chapter One).

As powerful players with close ties to governments, network operators can horse trade with regulators on these two principles of *intermediary liability* and *net neutrality*; for example, by offering the state greater control over internet traffic in exchange for less state control over their own business-related traffic management.

a local network), a *router* (which routes traffic between different networks), or a *firewall* (which controls access to computer *servers* for the purpose of network security).

A *network connection* is something that connects these nodes together somehow. It could be *wireless*, such as *wifi*, *3G* or *satellite*, or it could be a physical (*fixed line*) link between nodes, such as the *copper wire* typical of the first telephone networks, the *coaxial cable* typical of cable television in the US, or *optical fibre* cables that use pulses of light to transmit data at super-fast speeds.

Who shapes it?

Because the internet is a *network of networks*, the *physical layer* is controlled by lots of different network operators and internet service providers. They provide their customers with access to the entire internet by coming to arrangements with one another, either financial or in-kind, to exchange network access. In-kind arrangements (also called *peering agreements*) are executed at internet exchange points (*IXPs*).

"Network operators have a great deal of power over the data we transmit across their networks"

Network operators generally have close ties with the state. The largest *fixed line* network operators are either state-owned, or in the process of some kind of privatisation and/or market deregulation and consequently have a historic link to their governments. *Wireless* network operators also have close relationships with the state because their access to wireless frequencies (*spectrum*) is state-regulated.

What's at stake?

Network operators have a great deal of power over the data we transmit across their networks. They are under significant economic and political pressure to exercise that power, despite the existence of certain legal safeguards (see box on page 27).

The cost of investment in new physical infrastructure means network operators will underinvest in areas that are not seen to provide sufficient return, leading to a *digital divide* (See Chapter Five) between those with fast access and those with slow, or no, internet access. Pressure to maximise profits from existing infrastructure has left many network operators keen to experiment with new business models that, for example, offer different

UNDERSTANDING THE LAYER MODEL

	What is it?	Examples	Who shapes it?	What's at stake?
Content Layer	Information we access and share online	Text and images, data, video, voice, music	Users, from media and advertising companies to individuals	Hate speech; disinformation; copyright infringement; criminalisation of legitimate expression; defamation
Application Layer	Software that helps us access and share that information	Web browser, email client, social networking platform, search engine	Microsoft; Apple; Google, Facebook; free software developers; individuals	Censorship; surveillance; malware
Code Layer	Communications protocols	Internet Protocol (IP); Hypertext Transfer Protocol (HTTP); Domain Name System (DNS)	IETF; ICANN	Censorship through DNS seizure
Physical Layer	Network nodes connected by network connections	Computer, smartphone, server, switch, router, optical fibre, mobile phone base station	Network operators; internet service providers (ISPs); internet exchange points (IXPs)	Censorship through blocking and filtering; surveillance; net neutrality; the digital divide

online services premium access to their customers, threatening the end-to-end principle and *net neutrality.*

Network operators often find themselves the target of political, legislative or judicial campaigns to *filter,* or *block* access to, certain types of content (child sexual abuse images, inflammatory and copyright-infringing content, or material deemed seditious or indecent). Network operators are also under legal and extra-legal pressure to monitor their users' communications for the purpose of state surveillance. Both censorship and surveillance are accomplished using *deep packet inspection* technologies, probes that operate in the *code layer* (see next section), going beyond the *communications protocols* necessary for merely routing data and into the actual content of data *packets.*

THE CODE LAYER
What is it?

The *code layer,* also called the *protocol stack,* defines how the internet works. *Protocols* are technical standards – a bit like call and response patterns – designed to enable communications across a network. The different protocols in the protocol stack each enable a different aspect of communication across the internet, from how data is split into packets for transmission, and reassembled again, to how data packets are routed around the network. Together, the protocols in the protocol stack allow the internet to run on almost any type of physical infrastructure and carry any type of information.

The *protocol stack* includes the *communications protocols* that allow *network nodes* to locate one another on the internet. The most common of these communications protocols is the Internet Protocol (*IP*).

Who shapes it?

The technical standards that make up the *code layer* are overseen by the Internet Engineering Taskforce (*IETF*), an association of experts with no formal membership structure. At the IETF, *communications protocols* are developed, defined and standardised by specialist working groups, with an open invitation for anyone to participate. For more on the IETF, see Chapter Four.

The Internet Protocol (*IP*) relies on there being a large volume of unique numeric IP addresses. The maintenance of the IP address system is overseen by the Internet Corporation for Assigned Names and Numbers (*ICANN*), a non-profit private organisation constituted in the state of California. ICANN also oversees the management of *top level domains* and of the *root name servers* that operate the *domain name system* – the vital reference system that translates numeric IP addresses into human-readable names, and that is often likened to the telephone directory of the internet. For more on ICANN, see Chapter Four.

What's at stake?

Both *ICANN* and the *IETF* (through its parent organisation, the Internet Society) have their headquarters in the United States, and this has been the subject of significant international tension since the mid-2000s. However, since the remits of the IETF and ICANN are focussed squarely on technical good governance, this tension is best understood as symbolic: it represents a more generalised anxiety about US power on the internet, not least through the dominance of US corporations at the *application layer.*

The *domain name system* has been exposed as a point of censorship in recent years. *ICANN* delegates the operation of *Top Level Domains* (.org; .de; .co.uk, etc.) to *registries* that work with *registrars* to sell domain names (like "mywebsite.co.uk") to end users. Recently, government agencies, most notably the United States Immigration and Customs Enforcement agency, have acted to "seize" domains, by presenting their registrars with court orders to redirect (to US government *servers*) any traffic to websites they believe are trading in illegal or infringing information.

THE APPLICATION LAYER

What is it?

The *application layer* is made up of *software* that allows users to interact over the internet. It includes applications large and small, from the *browsers* (such as Internet Explorer, Firefox, Safari, Chrome), *search engines* (Google, Bing) and *social networking platforms* (Twitter, Facebook) of the *worldwide web*, to *email clients* such as Outlook and Thunderbird and *Voice-Over-IP* packages (Skype).

Who shapes it?

Whereas the *communications protocols* of the internet are rigidly specified and overseen by the *IETF*, anyone can create an application to run on the internet without asking for permission. Indeed, it is this feature of the internet that is most cited when people try to explain its rapid adoption and success, because it allowed companies like Google and Facebook to start small and to innovate in the market without needing to rely on the goodwill or cooperation of existing market players.

However, precisely because anyone can run code on the internet, computers connected to it are constantly at risk from viruses and *malware*. It was for this reason that many *smartphone* manufacturers made the decision early on in designing their products not to allow users the freedom to run whatever they liked on their smartphones. Instead they created *application stores*, like the Apple App Store, whose contents they cu-

THE FREE SOFTWARE MOVEMENT

Despite the prevalence of Google et al, the internet's end-to-end structure still allows important non-commercial players to occupy the *application layer*. Early on in the development of the internet, the *free software* movement recognised the fundamental role *software* would play in people's lives and worked to create alternative software, outside of corporate control, that was free to use, adapt and share.

The *free software* community is an activist community that seeks to protect users from censorship and surveillance, sometimes through advocacy but mainly through the development of free and transparent alternatives that avoid central points of control. They also help develop and maintain *software* to enable online anonymity (such as *TOR*) and software applications that help people encrypt their communications and data. Though small, this highly technical and motivated community is potentially an important ally for defenders of human rights.

rate, much like a shopkeeper would, to guarantee a minimum of security and quality.

Possibly also because of the prevalence of viruses and *malware*, as more and more people get online they have tended increasingly to rely on trusted brands. Today, the *application layer* is dominated by large commercial players: Google, Twitter, Facebook, Yahoo! and others. It is ironic that although the original internet was designed as a resilient network, not overly reliant on any one node for its success, market forces and so-called *network effects* have resulted in a situation where, when Google's *servers* went offline for two minutes in August 2013, they took 40% of the world's internet traffic with them.

What's at stake?

Most of the *application layer* giants, such as Google, Facebook and Twitter, are US-based (although in some cases, notably in China, it is local companies such as Baidu and Sina Weibo that dominate). Because these huge online companies interact with so many of the internet's users all around the world, they are attractive to governments as conduits for censorship and surveillance. Leaked United States National Security Agency (*NSA*) documents show that Apple, Facebook, Google, Microsoft, Yahoo! and others are all partners in the agency's PRISM surveillance program, responding to secret court orders for information on thousands of users' communications each year.

"Anyone can create an application to run on the internet without asking for anyone else's permission"

Facebook, Yahoo!, Microsoft, Twitter and Google all publish "transparency reports" – limited sets of data detailing some of the requests to censor content or provide user information that they receive from governments around the world, not all of which are complied with. This is a recognition of their growing role in the privatisation of censorship and surveillance online (See Chapter Five). These sites' own practices when devising and enforcing their terms of service can also have a general effect on free expression online, as their ever-increasing popularity cements their role as the "town square" of the internet.

Corporate social responsibility endeavours, such as the *Global Network Initiative*, which encourages internet companies to work with civil society groups to discuss ways to protect and promote the rights of their users, have come under significant pressure in the wake of the *NSA* leaks.

The *NSA* leaks have also resulted in calls from governments, such as those of Brazil and Germany, for US internet companies to store local data locally, rather than in the US. But it is not clear whether bringing citizens' data under the potential influence of their own governments will see local human rights activists better or worse off (see Chapter Six). Certainly, in repressive regimes where local internet giants dominate today, privatised censorship is the norm – China's Internet Society, a quasi-state body, gives annual awards for "Internet Self Discipline" to encourage companies to promote social and political "harmony" online.

THE CONTENT LAYER

What is it?

The *content layer* consists of all the information the internet's users share, publicly and privately, across the network – email, music, video, voice, links, photos and much, much more.

Who shapes it?

We all shape the *content layer*, with the information we share online. And we shape it in many different ways. Resources build up over time in online forums designed to serve communities of shared interest whose members may live far from one another. Government departments use the internet to make available vast stores of data about their operations, in efforts to promote transparency and accountability. The cloak of anonymity that the internet offers allows some people to find there the answers to problems that they are too scared to talk about in the "real" world, and others to launch campaigns of verbal abuse against people with whom they disagree.

What's at stake?

Although the actual technology of the internet places few limitations on the types of content that can be shared online, there are several sorts of legal restrictions, carrying various penalties, associated with sharing content online. These can have a chilling effect on free expression, especially when ordinary people are affected by laws that were intended to govern commercial publishers in a pre-internet age.

Copyright law is very important in this context. There have been instances of individual internet users being sued in the civil and criminal courts for sharing information that infringes copyright, and the big copyright interests have made agreements on the enforcement of copyright with network operators and major companies working in the *application layer*, such as YouTube.

"Today, ordinary people are affected by laws that were intended to govern commercial publishers in a pre-internet age"

Because copyright law protects a great deal of the information that is shared online, and because the free expression safeguards contained within copyright law are very nuanced, the misapplication of copyright law online can and often does result in censorship or the chilling of free expression. Despite this, governments around the world are being vigorously lobbied to strengthen their copyright laws, allowing for harsher punishments for infringers and more enforcement mechanisms for copyright holders.

Libel and defamation laws also apply to information that is shared online. The internet complicates these already complex laws further, because sometimes (on Twitter, for example) conversations between people who may feel they are speaking privately actually take place in public. The same can be said of decency and hate speech laws.

Although copyright and libel cases will usually be brought by individuals or companies, governments can also prosecute – and persecute – individuals for the content they share online. Governments across the world act to target people posting content that violates the law, often invoking computer misuse laws that bring harsher penalties for online speech than the same speech would attract offline. In many places, people posting content online that threatens the status quo are targeted by their governments as dangerous political dissidents.

And it's not just governments that make the law online. Network operators such as *ISPs*, and website operators such as Google and Facebook, ask users to comply with lengthy terms and conditions before they are allowed to access their services and share content. Those found violating the terms and conditions can be denied access in future.

chapter 4

CAN I SPEAK TO THE MANAGER?

Internet governance

The previous chapter introduced the players with the power to shape the internet and a stake in its future. Network operators can censor and monitor content at the *physical layer*. At the *code layer*, the *IETF* and *ICANN* set standards and maintain the key functions of the internet. The *application layer* is host to huge technology companies such as Google and Facebook, whose market dominance has conspired to make their services the "town squares" of the digital age. And, at the *content layer*, users themselves have the power to shape the internet, a power that comes with new dangers.

National governments of every stripe have, over the past two decades, developed ways of influencing and controlling the behaviour of these various stakeholders. Network operators and *application layer* service providers engage in censorship and surveillance of their customers on behalf of governments across the world, from the US to China and from Russia to Brazil. Frequently, this activity takes place in the absence of any statutory framework. In addition, new laws have been enacted that target user behaviours, often invoking legal concepts of computer misuse to ensure harsher penalties for online speech than for its offline equivalent.

Alongside this gradual taming of the internet by nation states, international debate about the global governance of the internet has raged. And although national governments still hold the keys to most of the human rights opportunities and challenges of the internet, it's important to understand the contours of this international dialogue, as the next few years are likely to see it gain more importance for human rights.

As the internet has come to affect more and more aspects of life across the world, pressure has built up to identify a way to deal with the challenges its global nature presents to state-level regulation (see box on page 43). Organisations with mandates as diverse as UNESCO and the G8 have begun to think about the internet and how to shape it. The last decade has seen escalating calls – particularly from countries in the developing world – for a global internet governance mechanism, able to set public policy norms. Opponents of such ideas fear that free expression and privacy standards would be calibrated to please the world's more authoritarian states. Proponents see in them the hope of spreading the internet's benefits more evenly across the globe. The international appetite for change has only been enhanced by revelations that the US, home to the major players at the *application layer*, and with ultimate dominion over *ICANN*, has been using the internet as its own private intelligence network.

> "Governments have developed ways of influencing the behaviour of those who have the power to shape the internet"

The UN sponsored two summits, in 2003 and 2005, to discuss these issues. These World Summits on the Information Society (WSIS 2003 and WSIS 2005, collectively know as the *WSIS process*) led to the establishment of the Internet Governance Forum (*IGF*), a group that has met annually since 2006, and that tries to bring together all the internet's stakeholders – users, network operators, government officials, technology companies and more. With the IGF's mandate set to expire in 2015, states are adapting diplomatic groupings and forming new ones in order to try and influence the future direction of debate, as well as attempting to table internet governance treaty proposals

42

IS GLOBAL INTERNET GOVERNANCE POSSIBLE?

Early internet pioneers defended the internet as a place that defied regulation, because of the network's global nature. Whatever laws individual states might impose, they argued, an internet user can always route around them. Since then, states have imposed many laws, aimed at network operators in the *physical layer*, at programmers, websites and service providers in the *application layer*, and at users in the *content layer*. But, at least where users have enough incentive and technical knowhow to share information that the state doesn't want them to share (whether they are teenagers sharing copyright-infringing copies of the latest Hollywood blockbuster, paedophiles sharing illegal images of child sexual abuse, or citizens of a repressive regime sharing information about their government), the vision of the early internet pioneers has remained largely intact. In short, no one ultimately governs the entire internet.

in multilateral settings and at the International Telecommunications Union (*ITU*) in 2012. Revelations concerning the extent of electronic surveillance undertaken by the spying agencies of the United States and its allies have lent even more urgency to the internet governance debate.

The internet governance debate is at a critical point, and the events of the next few years are likely to have a determining effect for decades to come. Human rights defenders have a unique opportunity to secure a positive future for human rights in a digital world, if they get involved now.

That future will be brighter if internet governance adheres to two principles. The first is multistakeholderism. The idea behind this odd-looking term is that, when it comes to internet governance, it is not only governments and corporations that have a stake: civil society needs to play an equally active role, helping to set the agenda and participating in meetings and discussions. This concept has existed since the beginning of the internet's history, when the *IETF* opened its doors for anyone to participate in standard-setting processes.

But although multistakeholderism is well-defined in relation to the technical governance of the internet, what it means in practice when negotiating policy-driven regulation – in particular ensuring plural and meaningful civil society participation, and deciding how much power business interests should be permitted to have – is far from clear. There is no single model of multistakeholderism, or agreement on what is an acceptable minimum level of civil society involvement. Nonetheless, multistakeholderism is widely endorsed, and so far, whenever governments have attempted to agree on shared approaches to internet governance behind closed doors (see the sections on *ITU* and trade negotiations, below), internet users have reacted with enough outrage to derail proceedings.

"The concept of multistakeholder governance has existed throughout the internet's history and is widely endorsed"

As we've seen in the previous chapter, the internet relies on the standard-setting processes at the *IETF* and the management of the *IP* address space and *Domain Name System* that is provided by *ICANN*. It's fair to say, therefore, that the technical governance of the internet is reasonably stable. The second principle that any international internet governance architecture must adhere to is therefore that it should not undermine the stability of the technical governance of the internet.

For the internet to remain both global and open (able to run on any type of infrastructure and carry any type of information) this second principle is crucial. It preserves what one of the original architects of "inter-networking" has called "permissionless innovation": the internet's trademark flexibility, and the open quality that has led to many of its benefits for human rights (the potential for bypassing state censorship, for example), as well as its rapid adoption worldwide.

The rest of this chapter explains the various forums in which internet policy-making is being discussed.

STATE-LEVEL GOVERNANCE

Governments still hold the keys to most of the human rights opportunities and challenges of the internet. Since the early 1990s, governments have enacted new laws and adapted old ones to attempt to regulate internet activity. Many of these laws focus on internet intermediaries, such as *ISPs*, and their legal liability for the information that travels across their networks. Most states compel intermediaries to *block* some types of content. Some, such as China, run complex censorship operations. Some states (the Netherlands, Chile) have legislated positively, to protect the fundamental design of the network through *net neutrality* laws.

Computer crime laws aimed at individual users have been strengthened for the internet age. Countries with tight media controls or strict public decency laws have attempted – sometimes successfully – to extend those laws to news websites, *social media* providers and even *social media* users. Laws protecting people's privacy and strengthening the protection of personal data also have the effect of regulating internet activity, as do copyright laws.

CORPORATIONS

The dominance of commercial players at every layer of the internet, but particularly at the *physical* and *application layer*s, makes the behaviour of a relatively small number of corporations increasingly crucial in shaping the internet landscape.

Beyond complying with laws set by nation states, corporations active in the internet space have responded to pressure from the governments of the countries in which they operate with various forms of self-regulation. Indeed, the fast-evolving nature of networking technology and internet applications has meant that industry self-regulation has often come to be seen as a preferred option by many states grappling with how to control people's behaviour online. The result of this trend is that civil society voices are often shut out of a sometimes too-cosy relationship between legislators and corporations.

Corporations, especially those at the *application layer*, such as Google and Facebook, have also responded to pressure from their users to act in a human-rights compliant manner, for example by issuing transparency reports detailing how they have responded to requests for user information from various governments, and by joining the *Global Network Initiative.*

USERS AND DIGITAL CIVIL SOCIETY

Because user satisfaction and user willingness to surrender personal information is central to the business models of application-layer giants such as Google (their motto, "Don't be evil", is designed to evoke user trust), it is important to them to be seen as user-centred organisations that act in a way that supports human rights. Users may therefore have more power to influence the behaviour of these corporations than might consumers of goods and services from companies operating at near-monopoly levels in other sectors.

Furthermore, the power of the internet as an organisational tool has meant that campaigns to promote human rights on the internet have benefited from high levels of participation from internet users. Over the past few years, mass online protest campaigns have steered a number of internet governance issues. In January 2012 an online "blackout" campaign spearheaded by Wikipedia and joined by an estimated 115,000 other websites, along with online petitions and nearly 10 million telephone calls made to legislators, served to shelve controversial online copyright enforcement legislation in the US. Similar protests also led the European Parliament to reject ACTA (see below) soon afterwards. In August 2012, after mass web blackout protests, the Malaysian government agreed to look again at legislation that threatened online expression.

Civil society groups dedicated to internet- and computer-related issues have existed since the mid-1980s. Some, such as Germany's Chaos Computer Club, have sprung from communities of computer programmers, and still do much of their work on technology-based issues and activism. The Electronic Frontier Foundation, founded by internet pioneers in the 1990s specifically to protect civil liberties online, works through legal cases and traditional advocacy. The number of digital civil liberties groups around the world is growing rapidly. Major international human rights NGOs are also slowly taking up digital civil liberties issues.

TECHNICAL GOVERNANCE

The following two organisations are broadly responsible for the internet's technical governance.

IETF

The Internet Engineering Taskforce (*IETF*) is an association of technical experts with no formal membership structure and an open invitation for anyone to participate. At the IETF, the *communications protocols* that power the internet at the *code layer* are developed, defined and standardised. The IETF operates through specialist working groups that use a system of written proposals called "Requests for Comment", and come to decisions on the basis of rough consensus.

The *IETF* does most of its work via email lists, and also meets three times a year. Although the IETF is a technical standard-setting body, it does make decisions that have an impact on internet users' human rights. For example, in its first meeting after the extent of US electronic surveillance via the National Security Agency (*NSA*) was revealed, it discussed making *encryption* part of a new web-browsing standard, a move that would offer some extra privacy protection for web users.

Nobody is paid to work with the *IETF*, although in practice the participation of many of the volunteers is subsidised by their employers: typically network operators, major website businesses, security firms and universities. The official corporate home of the IETF is the Internet Society (*ISOC*) which was founded for the purpose in 1992.

ICANN

The Internet Corporation for Assigned Names and Numbers (*ICANN*) manages the assignment of the *IP* addresses that allow computers to become part of the internet. It also oversees the management of *top level domains* and of the *root name servers* that operate the *domain name system*, which maps human-readable names to numeric *IP* addresses.

ICANN is a non-profit private entity constituted in the state of California. ICANN formally came into being in 1998 when it took over the duties of the Internet Assigned Numbers Authority (*IANA*), which worked under contract to the US government. The fact that ICANN is effectively US-controlled led to the disputes that kicked off the *WSIS* process in the early 2000s, since which time ICANN has tried to reform itself, allowing greater grassroots influence on its decision-making processes. Disputes over ICANN are broadly symbolic rather than substantial, related to wider anxieties among governments over how much public policy control they can have of the internet, and the dominance of US companies at the *application layer*.

THE UNITED NATIONS

The UN has played an important role in framing the debate around global internet governance. For example, the committees of the UN General Assembly have actively tackled internet issues, including cyber-warfare and internet access as a necessary dimension of the right to freedom of expression. The UN sponsored the *WSIS* process, which in turn led to the creation of the Internet Governance Forum (*IGF*). Several UN bodies are playing an active role in defining the future of this process once the IGF's mandate expires in 2015. Elsewhere, several of its agencies have also had key roles to play.

WSIS process and WSIS+10

The World Summit on the Information Society took place in 2003 in Geneva, and again in Tunis in 2005. It was a multistakeholder forum to discuss issues including internet governance. The Internet Governance Forum (*IGF*) was created as a direct result of *WSIS*. Follow-up meetings to assess the progress on issues discussed at WSIS have taken place in Geneva every year since, and a "High-Level Event", WSIS+10, took place in 2014.

IGF

The Internet Governance Forum (*IGF*) was set up by the UN in 2006 after the World Summits on the Information Society of 2003 and 2005 identified the need for a multistakeholder forum to discuss internet governance issues. It hosts a large annual meeting attended by governments, industry and civil society groups that discuss everything from the *digital divide* and cyber security to internet-enabled copyright infringement and the protection of children online. It has seeded a number of "dynamic coalitions" – informal groups that work together throughout the year – to examine issues such as gender, free expression and youth as they relate to the internet. Regional and national IGFs have also formed; they discuss issues of particular local concern and share their results.

"The UN has played an important role in framing the debate around global internet governance"

Although many have dismissed it as a talking shop with no real power, the *IGF* is the best example we have of what a multistakeholder policy forum looks like, and its open door to civil society participation makes it a useful forum for human rights activists.

UNHRC

The United Nations Human Rights Council (UNHRC) resolved in 2012 that "The same rights that people have offline must also be protected online". This was in part driven by the *Special Rapporteur* on the right to freedom of expression, and his report on free expression online. He has since produced a report arguing that online surveillance undermines free expression. UNHRC's Special Rapporteurs on the rights to peaceful assembly and freedom of association, and on contemporary forms of racism, have begun to engage with internet issues. Internet governance activists are also beginning to submit their own reports tracking online rights during the *Universal Periodic Review* process, which evaluates compliance with international human rights law in all UN member states.

CSTD

The Commission on Science and Technology for Development (CSTD) is a UN advisory group that has been tasked with making recommendations on internet governance and the continuation of the *WSIS* process once the *IGF* mandate runs out in 2015. It is due to report on these issues in 2014.

UNESCO

As part of its work, the United Nations Educational, Scientific and Cultural Organisation (UNESCO) promotes access to information and freedom of expression on the internet. It will help define the future for the *IGF*.

ITU

The International Telecommunication Union (*ITU*) is a specialised agency of the UN that promotes international cooperation on the use of radio and *satellite* communications, as well as trying to improve telecommunications infrastructure in the developing world. 193 member states participate in the ITU, together with 700 sector members, who pay an annual fee to participate. The ITU was the leading force behind the *WSIS* process and is now one of the facilitators for the WSIS+10 review process.

In 2012, the *ITU* attempted to update a telecommunications treaty that had last been agreed in 1988, proposing measures that would have had significant negative consequences for internet use. Civil society groups criticised the closed process surrounding the treaty negotiations and demanded a multistakeholder approach. Delegates from many European countries, the US, Japan and India refused to sign the revised treaty.

WIPO

The World Intellectual Property Organisation (WIPO) is another UN specialised agency, tasked with stimulating economic development and technology transfer through promoting creative activity. It is the home of international treaties on intellectual property, and agreed two "Internet Treaties" in the mid-1990s that aimed to strengthen copyright for the digital age.

WIPO came under pressure to reform during the 2000s and to recognise the complex role intellectual property law plays

in development issues. As a result, treaty negotiation processes are much more open than they once were, and civil society
observation and participation is welcomed: WIPO recently
agreed a landmark treaty securing exceptions to copyright laws
that will help visually impaired people share accessible reading
materials across borders. WIPO is currently negotiating a treaty
to establish a new kind of right for broadcasters and webcasters
that could dramatically restrict people's rights to share content
online.

COUNTRY GROUPINGS

Nations are adapting existing diplomatic alliances and
forming new ones to try and influence the future direction of
the internet governance debate. Some of these groupings try to
incorporate ideas of multistakeholderism in their operations. By
contrast, multilateral trade negotiations – where internet rules
are increasingly being discussed between sovereign states and
big business – intentionally leave civil society out in the cold.

The India, Brazil and South Africa Dialogue (IBSA)

IBSA is a "dialogue forum" for India, Brazil and South Africa. In 2011 it identified internet governance as a key strategic
area and endorsed a multistakeholder approach as well as a
greater role for the UN. Since the *NSA* revelations about extensive US surveillance of the internet, Brazil has emerged as a
leader on internet governance and hosted a multistakeholder
event on the issue, NETmudial, in April 2014.

OECD

The Organisation for Economic Cooperation and Development is a forum for cooperation between 30 member states
– mostly high income, developed economies – that seeks to promote economic progress and free market democracy. In Decem-
ber 2011 it produced a set of principles for internet policy-

making that encouraged multistakeholder cooperation in policy development processes.

Freedom Online Coalition

The Freedom Online Coalition is a group of 21 countries, and was launched by the Dutch government in 2011. These countries have made a commitment to protecting human rights online. The group includes the US, the UK, France, Estonia, Kenya and Tunisia.

The London Process/Conference on Cyberspace

Launched in London in 2011, this UK government-led forum has a strong emphasis on cyber-security and attracts Russian and Chinese participation.

Stockholm Internet Forum

The Stockholm Internet Forum is a multistakeholder event that first took place in May 2012. It aims to "deepen the discussion" on the relationship between online freedoms and economic development.

Trade negotiations (ACTA; TPP; TAFTA etc.)

The Anti-Counterfeiting Trade Agreement (ACTA), the Trans-Pacific Partnership (TPP) and the Trans-Atlantic Free Trade Agreement (TAFTA) all either contain or are suspected to aspire to conditions that would alter the way network operators police their networks and affect *intermediary liability*, mostly in the name of protecting intellectual property. Such provisions would have dramatic consequences for human rights, because they would set up privacy-invading systems on communications networks as standard, and have the potential to chill the free expression that relies on limitations and exceptions to copyright. The negotiation of these treaties takes place behind closed doors, and any civil society involvement is at best cosmetic. What's more, negotiators often share draft texts with corporate lobbyist "stakeholders" from their home countries, failing to acknowledge the effects the final agreements will have on ordinary internet users. As such, these treaties are increasingly the subject of suspicion and protest (see Users section, above).

chapter 5

WHAT A HUMAN RIGHTS ISSUE LOOKS LIKE NOW

A spotter's guide

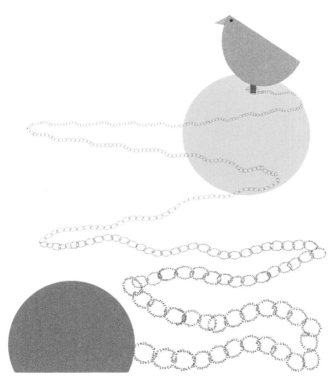

What it means to be a victim of censorship in the twenty-first century will be very different to what it meant in the twentieth. Even by the end of this decade, as access to the internet becomes widely accepted as a necessary dimension of the right to freedom of expression, so too might pervasive, always-on electronic surveillance be accepted as an inescapable reality.

Understanding how the internet affects human rights is understanding what human rights will look like in the future. And what human rights will look like in the future very much depends on whether those used to defending human rights in the past get involved now in defending them on the internet.

CENSORSHIP

Although overall the internet has been good for free expression, new forms of censorship have emerged. In particular, censorship has been privatised. Those acting to censor content online are usually private companies – network operators, online service providers etc. – censoring content either on behalf of a government (or governments) or in accordance with their own terms and conditions. Censorship committed on behalf of governments may be codified in law, or it may be the result of informal codes of conduct drawn up at industry roundtables in which civil society groups are not generally invited to participate.

Website-blocking and *website-filtering* happen when internet service providers (*ISPs*) either inspect and *filter* data *packets* for specified keywords (an important aspect of China's extensive online censorship system) or – as happens much more often – *block* access to specified web addresses. Who specifies the blocked keywords and web addresses then becomes the issue, and across the world there are different answers to that question. In many Middle Eastern countries, commercial website-blocking *software* is used, and lists of "political" or "indecent" websites are maintained by commercial companies such as the US company SmartFilter. In the UK, a list of child sexual abuse content that must be blocked by all ISPs is maintained by an industry-funded charity, the Internet Watch Foundation (see Harmful Content section, below). More recently, ISPs have received lists of web addresses to block from judges adjudicating in copyright infringement cases. In Russia, three different government agencies have the power, without any judicial oversight, to add web addresses to a blacklist. Russian ISPs are forced to block them in order to "protect the public".

"Those acting to censor content online are usually private companies"

Systems such as these run the risk of over-blocking, preventing access to legitimate content because it shares some features with the content that is the target of blocks. For example, blocking *software* intended to protect children from sexual material, such as China's abandoned Green Dam project (see box), and the mandatory *filtering* and "opt out" filtering currently proposed in Australia and the UK respectively may also affect the Lesbian, Gay, Bisexual and Transgender (LGBT) community, since discussion of sexuality can share some of the features of sexual content. This is particularly harmful to LGBT teenagers who want anonymity when seeking information about their emerging sexuality. In countries where the LGBT community is actively persecuted, denying access to information about sexuality becomes part of a broader picture of oppression.

CASE STUDY: A STEP TOO FAR? CHINA'S GREEN DAM

In 2009, Chinese authorities announced that from July that year, all computers sold in China should be shipped with new government-sponsored censorship *software* called Green Dam, purportedly developed to allow parents to limit their children's access to online pornography.

The Chinese online censorship system is the most elaborate in the world, incorporating extensive network blocking and keyword *filtering* at the *physical layer*, and requiring strict "self-discipline" from internet companies providing online services, which are bound by law to police their networks for any content posted by their users that might be detrimental to "harmony" (meaning the political and social status quo). The government also employs tens of thousands of people to monitor internet use and respond to critical posts online.

But even in this context, Green Dam – installed directly on the user's computer and linked back to the government in order to update block lists, but also (potentially) to send lists of web resources accessed – was a step too far. Public unease within China's borders was matched by an international outcry and diplomatic protests from the US. On top of this, the *software* was found to contain serious security vulnerabilities as well as large chunks of suspected plagiarised code.

The project to make Green Dam mandatory was put on hold – seemingly permanently – in August 2009.

Notice and takedown, first enshrined in the US Digital Millennium Copyright Act (*DMCA*) and later adopted in a slightly different form by the European Union in its *E-Commerce Directive*, is a legal framework intended to shield internet intermediaries such as *website hosts* or *social media* platforms (Facebook, YouTube) from legal liability for content that has been uploaded to their *servers* by web users. This law means that the intermediaries are obliged to take down content rapidly once they have been notified of allegations that it might constitute libel or be in some way illegal (EU), or infringe copyright (EU and US), This system is open to abuse, particularly in the EU where web users have little recourse if they feel their content has been taken down unfairly. The intermediary companies are much more likely to comply with notice and takedown requests than to challenge them.

Informal notice and takedown schemes also operate on most *social media* platforms, allowing users to report content they find offensive to the platform's operators. Such systems are also open to abuse because the companies operating the platforms do not tend to dedicate sufficient resources to resolving such complaints in a human-rights compliant manner (see box).

Notice and disconnection schemes, also called "three strikes" and "graduated response", are cropping up in some jurisdictions, as governments pass new laws compelling *ISPs* to respond to rights-holders' allegations of copyright infringement by writing to the users alleged to be involved and threatening to disconnect them from the internet. Such schemes have been condemned as disproportionate by the UN *Special Rapporteur* on free expression.

Network shutdowns, when governments and government agencies ask network providers to restrict access to network resources for a specified period of time, are growing in frequency. The Egyptian government ordered a network shutdown during

CASE STUDY: ARAB SECULARISTS ON FACEBOOK

There are over one billion different user pages (profiles) on the social networking site Facebook, more than any company could hope to police by itself. But Facebook does offer a way for users of its site to report abusive behaviour and violations of its terms and conditions, by filling in an email form.

The writer and campaigner Jillian C. York has pointed out that this system is heavily skewed against minority speech. For example, she details the case of a Moroccan Facebook user whose account was deactivated after he created a page calling for the separation of religion from education policy. Although Facebook refused to comment on the move, York linked it to another group on Facebook, whose name, translated from Arabic, is: "Together to close all atheist pages on Facebook", and which calls for its members to report the profiles of atheist users to Facebook as violations of its terms of service. York also tells the story of Najat Kessler, a US-based activist originally from Morocco, who believes her account was deleted after she made statements critical of Islam.

the protests that led to the ousting of President Hosni Mubarak. The Indian government has shut down mobile networks in various cities at times of civil unrest. The Pakistan government has switched off mobile phone networks in the Balochistan region of the country during key public holidays, claiming this was done in the interests of national security. Network shutdowns have also been reported in Syria and Sudan.

DDOS attacks are another novel form of censorship. Originally a tool of computer hackers, a distributed denial of service (DDoS) attack floods a network resource, such as a website host, with millions of fake requests that prevent bona fide traffic from accessing it. Reports of *DDoS attacks* against independent news media and human rights groups are common in Tunisia, Russia, China, Vietnam, Burma, Mexico, Israel, Egypt, and Iran. Government authorities and government-sponsored groups are often the perpetrators of these sorts of attacks, although DDoS is also the tool of choice for vigilante groups.

Clearly, the environment of online censorship differs radically from the terrain human rights defenders are used to. Because much of the online public sphere is controlled by private companies, censorship has been more or less privatised, and new free expression norms are being created at company HQs. The authority and depth of understanding possessed by human rights defenders are much needed in the forums where new rules affecting freedom of expression are being crafted: in industry self-regulatory bodies and at roundtable talks between government and industry.

SURVEILLANCE

The surveillance of networked communications and computers is fast becoming ubiquitous. Technological capability and political will are combining to create techno-legal frameworks with the potential fatally to undermine the human right to privacy, as well as the rights to free expression, freedom of association, and other rights.

The problem is that computers generally maintain a nearly indestructible record of what their users do – the websites they visit, the emails they send, the files they create. If the computer is a mobile *smartphone*, it also maintains a record of its user's movements. Once any computer is connected to the network, its record of user activity becomes vulnerable to attack not just at the physical location of the computer, but from any point across

CASE STUDY: FINFISHER

Finfisher uses a particular type of *malware* called a *trojan* to infect a computer with code that can monitor its user's activity without detection. The code can take screen shots, log keystrokes and intercept Skype calls, and transmits this information back to third parties for analysis. It also works on mobile phones, turning them into tracking devices.

Dissidents in Egypt have given accounts of being confronted with their own private text messages during interrogation sessions under the Mubarak regime. After the overthrow of Mubarak, they report finding a proposal from Finfisher's parent company, UK-based Gamma International, for supply of the *software*. There is evidence that Finfisher is in use in Australia, Bahrain, Bangladesh, Brunei, Canada, Czech Republic, Estonia, Ethiopia, Germany, India, Indonesia, Japan, Latvia, Malaysia, Mexico, Mongolia, Netherlands, Pakistan, Qatar, Serbia, Singapore, Turkmenistan, United Arab Emirates, the United Kingdom, the United States and Vietnam.

Privacy International have campaigned successfully to have Finfisher subjected to the export controls governing trade in military-grade technology.

the network. Any information sent across the network can be captured at some point along the way.

Governments across the world are exploiting this new reality. Revelations that the security services in the US, UK, Canada, Australia and New Zealand can legally access the electronic communications of nearly anyone on the planet have led to calls at the UN for human rights principles to apply to national security legislation. Syria, China, Iran, Bahrain and Vietnam stand accused of using similar techniques to target political dissidents and independent journalists.

The international surveillance market is worth $5billion and today's surveillance capabilities are eye-watering. Approaches range from tapping entire populations' communications as they flow through undersea *optical fibre* cables, to requiring internet and online service providers to maintain searchable records of all their customers' data, records that can be accessed by law enforcement and other government agencies. *Malware* that infects a target computer and uses it to spy on its users has been exported by Western companies to government authorities in Egypt and Bahrain. Small dummy mobile phone *base stations* known as *IMSI catchers* that can scan mobile phones in a 10km² area and identify and track their users have been purchased by London's Metropolitan Police.

The scale of the challenge is vast, but defenders of human rights are already involved in dialogues that seek to promote national security strategies that comply with human rights, and thus they have valuable expertise to share. They can also take advantage of their existing relationships with at-risk citizens to help protect them from digital communications surveillance.

THE GLOBAL DIGITAL DIVIDE

The social, political and economic potential of the internet can only be realised by people who have access to it. *Digital divide* is the term used to refer to disparities in access to the internet, Information Communication Technologies (ICTs) and ICT skills. Digital divides exist between different populations (rich and poor, old and young, men and women). The global digital divide is the difference in access to the internet and to ICTs between different countries.

The dimensions of the global *digital divide* are changing all the time, as governments stimulate investment in new connectivity schemes or as new technologies, such as *smartphones*, are rapidly adopted in parts of the developing world where *fixed line* access barely has a toehold. Broadly speaking, however, it is the developing world, and particularly sub-Saharan Africa, that is on the wrong side of the global digital divide. According to *ITU* figures published in 2012, of the bottom twenty countries as ranked by the number of people with access to the internet, twelve were in sub-Saharan Africa. Only one sub-Saharan country, the Seychelles, ranked in the top 100. At the bottom of the scale, Eritrea, East Timor, Burma, Burundi and Sierra Leone have 0.8-1.3% internet penetration, compared to 93-96% for Denmark, the Netherlands, Sweden, Norway and Iceland, the countries at the top.

The lack of physical infrastructure is the primary barrier faced by governments and citizens in countries on the wrong side of the *digital divide*. Because infrastructure and technology are expensive, particularly in rural areas, across large distances and difficult terrain, international institutions and governments have relied heavily on the private sector to invest in infrastructure and provide services. This market-centred approach has had limited success in much of the developing world. Recently, more progressive policy approaches, such as open access to infrastructure and airwaves, have begun to emerge.

There is much advocacy work to be done in the area of best policy practices around infrastructure. But there are other barriers to access besides the provision of infrastructure and services.

People also need to have the funds to be able to access the internet, and so the affordability of services and devices is a major challenge. In less developed countries, access to the internet costs around a third of average monthly incomes. In the developed world it costs only 2%.

The quality and speed of internet service affect the types of information that people can access. Statistics on the number of people accessing the internet in certain countries are misleading, because a country with seemingly high levels of internet access may have very slow internet speeds and poor-quality service. In addition, in countries where there is a high level of broadband access via mobile devices, the quality and speed of service will necessarily be lower, because mobile broadband (*3G*) speeds are much slower, and connectivity is more intermittent, than with fixed broadband. The kind of device being used to access the internet also affects the user's whole experience: mobile internet users tend to be consumers of information rather than creators. Along with other trends, this may add a new dimension to the gender divide, for example in communities where men access the internet via their personal computers (PCs) at work, while women access it via their mobile phones.

People need literacy and ICT skills in order to be able to make use of digital devices and services; they need content that is relevant and accessible to them, in a language and format appropriate to their way of life. This is particularly important for marginalised and vulnerable groups.

Human rights activists have an important role to play in trying to remove barriers to internet access, as it becomes increasingly fundamental to the realisation of people's general human rights. What's more, activists have a specific role in broadening discussions of internet accessibility beyond simple provision of access to the web, and encouraging acknowledgement of the specific needs of vulnerable and marginalised groups.

CASE STUDY: THE INTERNET WATCH FOUNDA-
TION AND CLEANFEED

The Internet Watch Foundation (*IWF*) is a UK organisation founded in 1996 after *ISPs* came under pressure from the government to do something to stop the circulation of images of child sexual abuse on the internet.

Today, as well as working with *ISPs* and the police to have any obscene content that is hosted in the UK taken down and its publishers prosecuted, the *IWF* manages a black-list of urls that host images of child sex abuse. It compiles this list from research and reports made by the public. ISPs in the UK are encouraged by the government to use the BT Cleanfeed *website-blocking* system to *block* all of the urls on this black-list, and about 95% of UK web traffic is now covered by Cleanfeed.

Although the *IWF* has successfully defended the black-list it maintains from political pressure to include more types of undesirable content, recent court cases in the UK have ordered *ISPs* to extend their use of the Cleanfeed system, so that it blocks copyright-infringing content. In this way a nation-wide blocking system that was established for the purpose of fighting patently illegal content is gradually being extended to cover more types of speech. Moreover, this process is taking place in the absence of any new legislation that would require democratic scrutiny and debate.

HARMFUL CONTENT

Much of the state-led policy discussion of internet governance centres around curbing the circulation of harmful content online. What constitutes harmful content is far from being a matter of consensus. Even where countries do agree about what they want to target, as they do in the case of images of child sexual abuse, they don't always agree about how. Civil society groups taking part in these discussions are concerned that any *website-blocking* systems that are set up to target harmful content risk being abused by governments seeking to curb legitimate speech (see Censorship section, above).

The lack of consensus about harmful content does not prevent extensive dialogue on the issue. Indeed, in the recent past there was much more discussion of harmful content and cybercrime in some internet governance forums than there was of surveillance, censorship and the *digital divide* – a reflection, perhaps, of the immediate concerns of the majority of the internet-using public.

At least on the English-speaking web, the cultural dominance of the United States and its radical free speech values mean that ethnic, religious and gender-based hate speech is only a click away (although major platforms such as Google do tend to comply with local hate speech laws; for example by excluding neo-Nazi content from search results for Google's French and German search portals).

More subtly, the illusion of anonymity that the web conjures can mean that racism, sexism and other forms of hate speech are quicker to surface online than they might in real life. Although many web users from disadvantaged groups report feeling empowered in the online sphere, many others report suffering acute levels of verbal violence and threats as social networking brings our virtual identities closer to our real-life ones.

chapter 6

STOP THIS THING,
I WANT TO GET OFF!

A changing world...

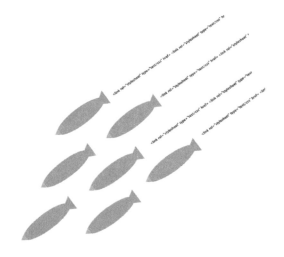

O̶ur digital society is evolving rapidly, driven by the development and adoption of the internet. It is tempting to think that we have for the most part already witnessed the extent of the disruption the internet will bring about. In fact, we are probably just at the beginning.

We cannot predict the effect of the internet on human rights in the future. But four near-term threats make the case for the immediate involvement of human rights defenders. Human rights defenders must get involved now in order to shape a future internet landscape that protects and promotes the values of international human rights.

WEAPONISATION OF CYBERSPACE

Evidence suggests that we are living in the early days of a cyber arms race. The US, UK and China are all investing heavily in the development of cyber-warfare capabilities. Examples of state-sponsored cyber-attacks already exist: *DDoS attacks* against Estonia in 2007 that brought down part of the country's banking system and were widely believed to have been sponsored by Russia; the Stuxnet *virus* (see box) that targeted Iranian nuclear facilities in 2010, believed to have been the work of the Israeli and US military.

The issue of cyber-security is undoubtedly a real one. But the steadily intensifying rhetoric surrounding cyber-security conflates many vastly different problems (harmful content, fraud, cybercrime, *cyber-espionage* and state-sponsored cyber-attacks) to create a sense of panic. This leads states to hand over large amounts of public money to the military-industrial complex and is used to justify their creation of all-pervasive surveillance systems.

There is a growing case for a cyber-demilitarisation movement, and human rights defenders have much to offer such a cause. As yet, no government has taken the lead in de-escalating the cyber arms race.

INTERNET BALKANISATION

In response to revelations about the extent of US surveillance online – aided and abetted by US companies, such as Google, Yahoo! and Facebook – governments, including those of Brazil and Germany, have called for the establishment of laws forcing companies that process the personal data of their citizens to keep that data within national borders, and encouraging regional internet traffic to be routed locally.

This has raised the spectre of a Balkanisation of the internet, an erosion of its global nature. China's Great Firewall, and the ambitions of the previous administration in Iran to build a "halal internet", have been invoked by people who fear that restrictions placed on the flow of information across borders will harm free expression. Although the harm to free expression is unlikely to be as dramatic as some people fear, if the policies proposed by Germany and Brazil were adopted widely, it would increase the costs of innovation online and potentially encourage authoritarian states to tighten their control of citizens' internet use further.

CASE STUDY: STUXNET

Stuxnet, first discovered in 2010, is a type of *virus* called a worm. It is designed to target specific industrial control systems, and it is widely reported to have been developed by the US and Israeli military to target Iranian nuclear facilities.

A number of computer *virus* experts have stated that Stuxnet appears to be the most sophisticated piece of *malware* to have become publicly known.

THE INTERNET OF THINGS

The gap between the physical world and the virtual world is closing. Tiny computer chips that can connect to increasingly ubiquitous *wireless* communications networks will soon give us the ability to enrol everything from parking meters to pacemakers into the *internet of things*.

The idea of an *internet of things* emerged just over a decade ago, with the concept of using radio-frequency identification (*RFID*) to allow computers to identify and track objects and people in the real world. RFID has since been adopted in the passports issued by many countries, and is widely deployed in the logistics operations of global retail businesses.

Today, ideas about the *internet of things* have evolved beyond the use of *RFID*, and encompass research on *human-computer interaction* that imagines humans surrounded by internet-enabled devices that can sense and respond to details and events without direct mediation – an environment of *ambient intelligence*.

Serious privacy concerns attend each of these visions of the future. In most cases, these technologies are being developed and deployed in a privacy-rights vacuum, without any significant analysis of their impact on human rights.

BIG DATA

Data is to the digital age as pollution was to the industrial age. As computers proliferate, the data they produce multiplies. For example, our entire individual spending records and web browsing histories – maintained and guarded (we hope) on our behalf by credit card companies and *ISPs* – are the tip of the data iceberg. Fitted with *GPS satellite* navigation, our cars remember where we have driven. A network of sensors takes 1.5 million readings of the oceans' temperatures each month. Twitter posts 400 million tweets per day. An electronic stock exchange records millions of trades per second.

Businesses and governments are increasingly recognising the value in harvesting and analysing data, in order to improve the products they sell us and the way they govern us. Big data is the new business buzz word. Many governments are publishing online datasets – for example, on water quality, employment, or spending – in forms that invite non-profit and commercial players to evaluate and exploit them. Some countries with national health services harbour ambitions to use the confidential electronic health records of their populations to transform themselves into global centres of industrial medical research.

Alongside data comes data analysis. *Algorithms* shrouded in trade secrecy deliver our search results, and increasingly also verdicts on our creditworthiness or even eligibility for state benefits. Predictive policing, which uses data on crime to allocate police resources, and even to target potential criminals before they have committed any crime, is already a reality in some cities. Behind these innovations is a subtle shift: from a society putatively governed by ethics and moral judgement to one based on number-crunching.

The conflicts between this vision of the future and one that respects our rights to privacy and freedom from discrimination are unresolved. Claims that data can be sufficiently anonymised to prevent harm to individuals do not stand up to scrutiny. The issues of mechanised discrimination that will inevitably crop up in this new world remain largely unexplored.

GLOSSARY

How to speak geek

3G — Short for "third generation". A type of mobile communications technology.

algorithms — A process or set of rules that a computer follows in order to complete a calculation.

ambient intelligence — A phrase intended to conjure up a future in which ubiquitous computing and pervasive data collection create smart environments that respond to their occupants.

application layer — In the context of the layer model of the internet (see Chapter Three), this layer is made up of software that allows users to interact over the internet.

application stores — Or "App stores". Interfaces that permit access to software applications providing additional functions on smartphones, curated to a greater or lesser extent by the creators of smartphone operating systems.

base stations — Networking hardware associated with mobile phone networks.

block	To prevent users from accessing a particular web url or other internet resource.
browsers	Software that allows users to navigate the worldwide web.
coaxial cable	A type of fixed line network connection, typical of cable television in the US.
code layer	In the context of the layer model of the internet (see Chapter Three), the layer made up of communications protocols that together permit the internet to function on almost any hardware and carry almost any type of information.
communications protocols	Technical standards – a bit like call and response patterns – designed to enable communications across a network.
content layer	In the context of the layer model of the internet (see Chapter Three), the top layer of the internet, made up of the text, images, voice, code and other data shared by the internet's users.
copper wire	A type of fixed line network connection typical of the legacy telephone network.
cyber-espionage	Spying activities carried out across communications networks.

DDoS attacks	Distributed Denial of Service attacks. The act of preventing access to an internet resource by flooding it with bogus requests. Attacks are "distributed" in the sense that all these requests purport to come from different locations, making them hard to block.
deep packet inspection	A type of content filtering found in the code layer, which, rather than only examining the communications protocols necessary for routing the data, also looks at the content of those data packets. Carried out by network operators, often for the purposes of surveillance and censorship.
digital divide	Unequal access to the internet between different groups of people.
DMCA	Digital Millennium Copyright Act, a piece of US legislation that, among other things, established the concept of intermediary liability.
DNS seizure	The attainment by a government agency of a court order to seize a web domain on the basis that the operator of that domain is engaged in criminal activity. The warrant is presented to the registrar of the domain, who must then make alterations preventing requests for that domain name from reaching the corresponding numerical IP address (see Domain Name System) of the computer engaged in the criminal activity.

Domain Name System (DNS)	The telephone directory of the internet, it links numerical IP addresses to human-readable addresses.
E-Commerce Directive	European legislation that brought the concept of intermediary liability, originally established by the DMCA, to Europe.
email clients	Software interface used for email access (e.g. Outlook, Thunderbird).
encryption	Encoding data to prevent third parties who might intercept it from being able to read it.
to filter	To inspect data packets for key words and block or re-route traffic containing the specified terms.
firewall	Software or hardware that controls access to computers for the purpose of network security. Used figuratively in the phrase "Great Firewall of China" to denote the extensive Chinese online censorship system.
fixed line	A type of networking connection involving physical infrastructure as opposed to radio- or micro-waves.
free software	Software that users are free to examine, copy, adapt and share.
Global Network Initiative (GNI)	Internet and telecoms industry self-regulatory body that works with civil society groups to establish principles for protecting human rights online.

GPS	Global Positioning System. Satellite-based navigation system that provides location information.
human-computer interaction	Study of the relationship between humans and computers.
IANA	Internet Assigned Numbers Authority. The department of ICANN that oversees IP address allocation, formerly controlled by the US government.
ICANN	The Internet Corporation for Assigned Names and Numbers. Governance body that oversees the allocation of IP addresses and manages the Domain Name System.
IETF	The Internet Engineering Taskforce, the body responsible for setting the technical standards at the code layer of the internet.
IGF	Internet Governance Forum. A multistakeholder forum for discussing internet governance. The IGF emerged from the WSIS process.
IMSI catcher	A piece of surveillance equipment, disguised as a mobile phone base station, and designed to discover identifying information (for example, the unique IMSI, or International Mobile Subscriber Identity number) of mobile phones in a specific area.

intermediary liability   A legal term denoting the levels of liability that internet intermediaries, such as network operators, web hosts and social media platforms, must legally assume for content that travels along their wires or that is uploaded to their servers and platforms.

internet of things   Phrase used to conjure a future where, in much the same way as internet resources have IP addresses now, physical objects and people will have unique identifiers that can be tracked by computer.

IP   Internet Protocol. Part of the protocol stack, it allows computers to enrol themselves on the internet and allows other computers to find them.

ISOC   The Internet Society, corporate home of the IETF.

ISPs   Internet Service Providers. Organisations that provide access to the internet and (commonly) operate parts of the network that make it up.

ITU   The International Telecommunications Union. A specialised agency of the UN that promotes international cooperation on the use of radio and satellite communications, as well as trying to improve telecommunications infrastructure in the developing world.

IWF	Internet Watch Foundation. A UK industry-funded charity that maintains a black-list of child sex abuse images to which UK ISPs block access.
IXPs	Internet Exchange Points. Locations for ISPs to execute peering agreements, granting their customers access to parts of the network they themselves do not operate.
malware	Malicious code designed to compromise someone's computer.
modems	A device that modulates digital data into an analogue signal that can be carried along a telephone wire.
net neutrality	The principle that network operators should not discriminate between data packets they carry across their networks. Net neutrality underpins the fundamental design of the internet: the end-to-end principle.
network connections	Connections between nodes on a communications network. They can be wireless or fixed line.
network effects	The effect that one user of a commodity or service has on the value of that good or service to other people. Describes the phenomenon whereby the more people use a particular service, the more people are likely to use it.

network nodes	In a communications network, nodes are the individual computers, servers and network hardware. Nodes are connected to each other by network connections.
network of networks	A phrase used to describe the internet, and its origin in the "inter-networking" of various packet-switching networks developed across the US and Europe.
network shutdowns	The act of "switching off" access to communications resources across an entire country or region.
notice and disconnection	Also called "Three strikes". A graduated response from an ISP to alleged illegal or infringing activity by an internet user. This might begin with letter-writing and end with the user being disconnected from the internet.
NSA	National Security Agency, a US spy agency recently revealed to be complicit in pervasive electronic surveillance activity.
optical fibre	A type of network connection that transmits data at super-fast speeds using pulses of light.
packet-switching	A resilient networking method that, rather than relying on a communications channel being open for the duration of a message transmission, separates communications into chunks (packets) and routes them on a first-come, first-served basis.

packets	Chunks of data routed around a packet-switching communications network.
peer-to-peer file-sharing	A way of sharing information that does not rely on it being stored in a central resource.
peering agreements	Contracts negotiated between ISPs to exchange access to networking infrastructure.
physical layer	In the context of the layer model of the internet (see Chapter Three), the bottom layer of the internet, made up of physical networking hardware.
protocol stack	The code layer of the internet. The layer made up of communications protocols that together permit the internet to function on almost any hardware and carry almost any type of information.
protocols	Technical standards – a bit like call and response patterns – designed to enable communications across a network.
registry	A database of all domain names within a given top level domain, containing information about who has registered them and which computers (for example, one hosting a website) the registrant has requested they point to.
registrar	An organisation that manages the registration of domain names.

RFID	Radio-Frequency Identifier, a technology that allows computers to communicate with physical objects. It underpins the concept of the internet of things.
root name servers	The limited number of computer servers that operate the backbone of the domain name system.
router	A piece of networking hardware that forwards data packets around a network.
satellite	A type of network connection using hardware that orbits the Earth.
search engines	A web service designed to locate resources on the web using search terms. The most popular is Google.
server	A computer that hosts content on the internet, such as emails or websites.
smartphones	Mobile phones with superior computing power.
social media	See social networking platforms – Twitter, Facebook, Sina Weibo, LinkedIn, YouTube.
social networking platforms	Websites, such as Facebook and Twitter, the primary purpose of which is to connect people online and the content of which is the contributions made by their users.

software	The programs used by a computer, including those programs designed to operate and control the computer hardware (such as the operating system) and applications software (such as word processing suites).
Special Rapporteur	In the context of the UN Human Rights Council, an independent expert who works on behalf of the UN under various thematic mandates. Often tasked with conducting research and undertaking fact-finding missions.
spectrum	Used in the context of communications to denote radio spectrum – the portion of the electromagnetic spectrum used for radio communication, including television broadcasting, mobile phones and satellite communication.
switch	A piece of networking hardware that links and routes network traffic between hosts on a local network.
TCP/IP	TCP/IP is short for Transmission Control Protocol/Internet Protocol, but it is almost always referred to in the abbreviated form. It is also known as the protocol stack. A series of communications protocols that together permit the internet to function on almost any hardware and carry almost any type of information.
Top Level Domains	The part of the domain name at the end of a url; for example, .com, .co.uk, .nl .

TOR	The Onion Router. A system enabling users to communicate anonymously over the internet.
trojan	A type of computer virus that delivers malicious computer code hidden inside something else.
Universal Periodic Review	A mechanism of the UN Human Rights Council through which member states undergo periodic examination of their human rights records.
url	Uniform Resource Locators. The human-readable text used to locate something on the internet; for example, website.com.
virus	Malicious computer code capable of copying itself. Viruses destroy data or have some other negative effect on their host computers.
voice-over-Internet Protocol	Or VOIP: internet telephony.
website hosts	Organisations or individuals that run computer servers hosting websites.
website-blocking	Preventing access to a web url or other internet resource.
website-filtering	Inspecting data packets for keywords, in order to block or re-route traffic to websites containing specified terms.
wifi	A type of wireless networking connection.

wireless	A type of networking connection involving radio communications spectrum of some kind (mobile, wifi, satellite).
worldwide web	A system of interlinked files and documents on the internet, navigated using a web browser.
WSIS and WSIS process	The World Summits on the Information Society, held in 2003 and 2005, and the activity since then to monitor the outcomes of the resolutions made at these summits.

ABOUT THE AUTHOR

Becky Hogge is a UK-based writer and campaigner and the former Executive Director of the Open Rights Group. She is a member of the UK telecommunications regulator (OfCom)'s Advisory Committee for England, and sits on the Advisory Councils of the Open Rights Group, the Foundation for Information Policy Research and the Open Knowledge Foundation.

Her writing on information politics, human rights and technology has been published by *openDemocracy.net*, the *New Statesman*, the *Guardian*, *Index on Censorship*, *Prospect*, the *New Scientist* and the *Atlantic*. Her first book, *Barefoot into Cyberspace: Adventures in search of techno-Utopia*, was published in 2011. She blogs at http://www.barefootintocyberspace.com.

ACKNOWLEDGEMENTS

The contents of this book were originally commissioned by Global Partners Digital in the run up to NETmundial, the Global Multistakeholder Meeting on the Future of Internet Governance, held in São Paulo, Brazil, in April 2014.

The author wishes to thank Dixie Hawtin, Andrew Puddephatt and Rebecca Zausmer at Global Partners Digital for their advice and input, as well as James Casbon for technical assistance. Thanks also to Patrick Casbon for assistance during the typesetting process. Any errors remain the responsibility of the author.

Lightning Source UK Ltd.
Milton Keynes UK
UKOW06f2248240715

255772UK00011B/133/P